ETOSHA

Rhythms of an African Wilderness

ETOSHA

Rhythms of an African Wilderness

Written by Claudia du Plessis
Photographs by Claudia & Wynand du Plessis

For Julia
and all children of the world

We hope that nature will find a place in their hearts, and that during their lives there will still be wildernesses,
which they may explore, experience and love.

We would like to thank the following people, whose support helped this book become a reality:

Iris Daschner and Rudolf Wittmann for their superb editing of the German text; Wilfried Auer, Norbert Schmid
and Martin Gabriel for their tireless proof-reading of the German edition; Ginger Mauney and Jan le Roux
for their valuable revision of the English edition. Thank you very much indeed.

Contents

Preface

He flicked his tail nervously.

A dignified female lay beside him and watched calmly as he rose, took the first steps towards us and then accelerated to a full charge within a few seconds. His powerful muscles moved rhythmically. The massive paws kicked up dust and sent small pebbles flying high into the air. His golden and black mane blew about wildly in the wind. Every centimetre of the thoroughly fit and massive body was in motion but for one exception: his ochre-coloured eyes. During the entire charge he kept his piercing gaze fixed on us without blinking even once. His head grew larger with every leap. When his face finally filled the camera's viewfinder I screamed: "Wynand, GO, GO, GO!!!"

Moments later there was a metallic bang: the lion hit the back of the vehicle with his front paws, and our hearts stopped beating. Then at last, "Lola" our Land Rover, puffing and panting, picked up enough speed and got away. Through the rear window I saw the magnificent prime male lion slowly come to a halt. After throwing a last glance at us, he leisurely returned to his mate and flopped down beside her.

Still trembling from the surge of adrenalin and speechless with the intoxicating mixture of excitement and fright, we stopped the car at a safe distance. "Mad Max", as this lion was named later after he had charged vehicles repeatedly, had clearly shown us that he would not tolerate humans nearby when he was with a female in heat – when "love was in the air". Gradually we relaxed. At the same time a different feeling, a kind of inner warmth, came over us and began to flow through every cell of our bodies: that of deep awe mixed with great enthusiasm. We felt stunned by the lion's primeval strength and power. His perfect beauty had touched our very souls.

To this day the feelings of awe and enthusiasm remain, spilling over to the numerous other wild creatures that have crossed our paths in the many years of living in Etosha. With each day we have spent in the magic world of the wild these feelings have deepened and grown into an enduring love for Etosha and the countless wonders of nature.

With our photographs and experiences we would like to give you, dear reader, an insider's understanding of Etosha, hoping that our passion and love for this and other wild places of the world may inspire you too.

Etosha National Park

Wild Place of Contrasts

It is midday. Silence lies over the land; in the numbing heat all life seems to be holding its breath. Through binoculars, we watch tiny, dark shapes, seemingly trembling in mid air above the vast expanse. Beyond, earth and sky melt into one another like watercolours, the horizon dissolves into nothingness. In the distance there is a shimmer like water, but the shapes move past it and towards us in a shivering dance. Slowly they come closer, continually growing in size, until they finally take clear shape: they are Burchell's zebras. With heads nodding, they walk in single file, following ancient game paths across a vast, open plain: the Etosha Pan, the heart of Etosha National Park.

Situated in Northern Namibia, the Etosha Pan extends over an area of 4 760 square kilometres and from the air, it resembles a giant footprint. One hundred and ten kilometres long and 60 kilometres wide, the Etosha Pan is a one and a half metre thick layer of sediments, which lies on top of solid silt and clay bedrock. During the dry season the pan floor breaks up into a mosaic of millions of small clay blocks, which are covered with fine salt crystals and gleam white in the glistening sunlight. Mostly barren and flat, the Pan is the ideal stage for mirages; created by movements of warm air rising, they distort the familiar beyond recognition and feign distant lakes.

The "White Sea", as the Heikom Bushmen, the original inhabitants of Etosha, call the Etosha Pan, is dry for most of the year. But in years of good rain we have seen the Pan turn into a shallow ephemeral lake, changing from a desert into an oasis. Then, thousands of flamingos flock together from afar to feed, mate and nest on this short-lived paradise.

For a long time the Etosha Pan was thought to be a desiccated ancient lake. However, recent research disputes this theory and suggests that the Pan originated from erosion over the past two million years. According to these findings, precipitation weathered the base rock in every rainy season, and strong winds blew out fine, weathered material in the following dry season. In this way rock was removed during the continuous cycle of seasons, lowering the Pan by two to five metres, a process that still continues today. Therefore, the distinct landform of the Etosha Pan, which is clearly visible from outer space, is the result of the powerful force of the natural elements in Namibia's semi-arid climate.

The Etosha Pan lies imbedded in a sea of vast savanna landscape, for which it holds a priceless jewel: along its edge, where it has cut into the bedrock, spring water trickles out in a number of places and forms life-giving pools. This is where the zebras we have been watching were headed, and where thousands of other park inhabitants like springbok, blue wildebeest and gemsbok gather to drink, day after day in the dry season. Thus, the desert-like Etosha Pan is paradoxically the heart and life-blood of one of the world's greatest wilderness areas, the Etosha National Park.

The Etosha National Park is an island of wilderness, separated and protected from surrounding fields, farm animals and settlements by a partly game-proof fence. With the impressive size of 22 970 square kilometres, half the size of Switzerland, the Park is home to more than 65 000 large mammals. Amongst these are approximately 25 000 springbok, 8 000 gemsbok, 10 000 Burchell's zebras, 3 000 blue wildebeest, 2 000 giraffes, 6 000 greater kudus, 1 000 red hartebeest, 1 500 black-faced impalas and 1 500 eland.

Etosha's open grass plains and extensive shrub and tree savannas offer a variety of different habitats. One hundred and fourteen mammal species occur here, including charismatic animals such as the African elephant, the black and white rhino, the lion, leopard and cheetah. Over 340 bird species have been counted in Etosha, many of which are migratory, visiting and leaving with the seasons, and numerous reptiles, amphibians and insects are part of the Park's fauna too.

A visit to Etosha is unforgettable. The almost unimaginable vastness overwhelms; the aura of tranquillity and peace radiating from the grazing antelopes that dot the yellow plains, enchants; and the untamed wildness with which a herd of elephants storms a waterhole touches the soul deep within. The power of wild nature that is felt here catapults one back into a time when man was still insignificant and nature ruled the earth. It is reminiscent of Africa when it was still relatively untouched and when bountiful wildlife roamed the continent freely.

Etosha's pronounced seasonal changes strongly affect its wildlife. During the rainless months of the southern winter, from May to August, clear skies take the land below on a temperature seesaw. High day temperatures of almost thirty degrees Celsius alternate with cold nights of nearly zero degrees. The dryness deprives the plants of moisture, forcing most herbivores to drink regularly.

From September to December the sun climbs higher each day. The day temperatures increase beyond the bearable and warm nights hardly bring relief. The land becomes desolate. In the dry, hot air, the vegetation withers and the waterholes dwindle rapidly. For the wildlife the search for food becomes more arduous and the daily walk to the remaining waterholes longer and harder. When almost all hope for relieving rain is lost, a breeze of moist air announces that the summer rains are on their way.

Around January massive thunderclouds build up over most of Etosha and burst at last in magnificent storms. The long-awaited rain drowns the parched landscape, renews the vegetation and replenishes the waterholes. In large, mixed herds, the herbivores gorge themselves on fresh, green grass and soft, young leaves of trees and shrubs. Along the way they drink freely at the countless rainwater pools. This is the season of abundance for Etosha's wildlife, a precious time for renewal and regaining strength before the return of the long and hard dry season.

In the Etosha National Park the seasons take the wildlife on a roller coaster from heaven to hell, but the animals have adapted well to this over thousands of years. For us humans, however, Etosha is an exhilarating experience in each season, an unforgettable encounter with the wild and its countless secrets.

In the heart of the Etosha National Park lies the Etosha Pan, a vast expanse of silt and clay sediments. During the dry season the pan floor breaks into a mosaic of small clay blocks, which swell during the rainy season and turn into sticky mud. After days of heavy rain the Pan may even be covered by a thin sheet of water, resembling a vast lake. Whether wet or dry, the barren Pan remains a favourite retreat for gemsbok (above), Burchell's zebras (page 7) and other wildlife away from lurking predators.

Numerous springs emerge along the Pan's edge, attracting a multitude of wildlife. Heading there for a refreshing drink a group of kudu females halts nervously and scans the long grass for any hidden danger.

Full bellies like these tell that there is nothing to be feared right now from this lion couple. At Okondeka spring they are quenching their thirst after a nightly meal and will soon head for a shady spot to relax for the rest of the day.

Thousands of animals may visit Okaukuejo (above) and other waterholes on a single day during the dry season. The various game species usually drink peacefully together. When the animal pressure is high, however, competition for drinking space is fierce. Here, springbok and other smaller animals often wait patiently for hours for their chance to drink (bottom right and top right) after dominant species, like elephants and gemsbok (far right), have moved off.

Lions, black rhinos and elephants are charismatic animals and are undoubtedly amongst Africa's most popular wildlife species. Once common throughout southern Africa, excessive hunting and poaching during the past 150 years for skins, horns and tusks brought their numbers down drastically. Today these animals have a safe haven in Etosha and other protected areas.

Etosha's lions are unique amongst the African lions. They are the only population on the continent that is free of FIV (Feline Immunodeficiency Virus), the feline equivalent of HIV in humans.

Black rhinos have suffered severely from poaching. With only 2 700 free-ranging individuals left worldwide, they are threatened with extinction. Therefore nature conservation authorities in Etosha pay special attention to them.

Compared to their relatives in eastern and southern Africa, Etosha's elephants have relatively short and brittle tusks. This is due to a mineral deficiency in their food and water. Ironically, it has created a life saving flaw, as their tusks are less valuable on the black market and therefore less desirable to poachers.

Etosha holds a diversity of wildlife including black-faced impalas, graceful antelopes that are only found in north-western Namibia and south-western Angola. Favouring shrub and woodlands, black-faced impalas occur in large herds of ewes and their offspring. The males, with their long, distinctive horns, remain single or in bachelor groups for most of the year.

The giraffe, the tallest land mammal, specializes by feeding on leaves at the tops of trees, where other browsers cannot reach. With its extensive mixed woodlands the east of Etosha is home to a large number of giraffes.

As the fastest animal on earth, reaching top speeds of 112 kilometres per hour, the cheetah is a very successful hunter that favours Etosha's grass plains and shrub savannas. Yet it is also the most delicately built of all the big cats and loses many a kill to lions, spotted hyenas and leopards. Moreover, the cheetah is the only predator in Etosha commonly dying from anthrax, a bacterial disease that occurs naturally amongst the Park's wildlife. Pressure from other predators and anthrax are thought to be responsible for the low number of cheetahs in Etosha, which is currently estimated at 100 individuals.

Besides the spectacular large animals, Etosha is home to a number of small mammal species, as well as a variety of birds, reptiles, amphibians and insects. Each of these animals plays an important role in the ecology of Etosha.

With some luck and a keen eye, the observant visitor may encounter young Cape foxes, tree mice, the helmeted guineafowl, the yellow mongoose, warthogs, the Damara dik-dik and perhaps even the shield-nose snake (clockwise from top left).

Amongst the diversity of life in the park are also the black korhaan, the leopard tortoise, the blackshouldered kite, the scrub hare, whitefaced owls and the ground squirrel (clockwise from top left).

19

Etosha and its wildlife experience dramatic changes between the seasons. The dry season with its extreme heat, drought and shortage of food (left) brings many animals to the edge of survival before the rainy season finally sets in and brings relief (right). Then, for a brief period of time, food and water are abundant (below) and all life regains its strength before the long, hard dry season returns.

Clear Skies Above

The Cool Dry Season

- May to August -

A cloud of white dust

obscures most of the action, but the growls and snarls tell me that this is a fierce struggle. Now and then I catch glimpses of what is happening: Three massive male lions have sunk their teeth into a dead zebra foal and pull and tug at it with all their might, each one in a different direction. Suddenly, the lifeless body tears and one lion breaks away with half of the foal. At a safe distance he devours the kill greedily with a few bites, while the other two continue their struggle. Gradually tiring in the warm midday sun, their tugging becomes weaker, until they eventually lie down, still holding on to the zebra and snarling softly now and then. Finally one of them gives up, leaving the tiny piece of meat – no more than a mouthful – to his rival, and joins the lionesses resting in the shade.

Since the cold morning hours, eight lions have been dozing and waiting near the spring of Okondeka. They are expecting the herds of animals that will be streaming in during the course of the morning. Come they will, this is as sure as sunrise. In the rainless months of the dry season the rain water pools have long dried up and the withering grasses and leaves contain less and less moisture. Now the remaining perennial waterholes are vital for those driven by thirst. Every day large herds of blue wildebeest, Burchell's zebra, springbok, gemsbok, red hartebeest, black-faced impala, giraffe and greater kudu come for a drink. Many of them start out on their journey to the water well before sunrise, and some will have walked up to ten kilometres by the time they finally take their first sip.

The sun had begun to climb the clear sky and to warm the air when some of the lions, their eyes fixed upon the horizon, got up as if on cue and fanned out quietly. Near a well-trampled game path they lay down, each in a different spot behind yellow tufts of grass. Their coats and the drying vegetation blended together, providing perfect camouflage. Through my binoculars I made out the first herds of zebra, wildebeest and springbok walking in files across the open plains. They slowly drew near, while the mighty cats lay motionless in wait, hardly noticeable. Only now and then a lion would lift its head cautiously above the grass tops to take a peep at the prey, or a black-tufted tail would twitch nervously. From all directions animals were moving to the water. Some groups came relatively close to the lions, but not near enough for a successful charge. The minutes passed, two hours went by – the lions remained waiting.

Finally, with heads hanging low a herd of wildebeest drew near in a steady plod. The lions crouched down with gazes fixed and bodies tensed, awaiting the right moment. As the wildebeest came within reach, the leading bull stopped dead in his tracks, and behind him all the others came to a halt. Some clue, perhaps a faint smell or a twitching ear, had made him suspicious. Yet, he wasn't certain. For a while the herd stood there indecisively, some stamping their forelegs nervously, others flicking their tails, while their eyes scanned the terrain ahead and their ears listened out for sounds betraying a threat. The air was loaded with tension when suddenly, a loud

snort rent the silence. One wildebeest had detected the slight movement of a lioness creeping carefully towards them. Outraged snorts echoed back and forth amongst the herd; they turned around in a split second and galloped off with waving manes and thundering hooves.

My eyes followed the wildebeest through the binoculars: they kept on running in a wide curve until they reached the glistening band of shallow spring water, that stretches far out onto the Etosha Pan. At the water's edge they stood next to each other and began to drink in large gulps. It was late morning and the spring was bustling with activity: zebras chased each other in boisterous play, zigzagging through snoozing wildebeest, scattering springbok that had approached wearily and spooking ostriches that had been strutting about with their feathers puffed up. A curious black-backed jackal trotted cheekily towards an Egyptian goose that had been swimming with its three chicks at the water's edge. Distrusting the jackal's bold approach, the goose now hurried off, hissing indignantly, to get its family to safety.

A little way off from the waterhole it was quieter. In the shade of the few trees small groups of animals were resting during the warm midday hours. Soon they and the other herbivores would set off again back to their feeding grounds. Later, in the evening and at night it is quieter at the waterhole with only predators visiting occasionally.

The lions were still lying in wait, when a herd of zebra came along, heading straight for them. Totally oblivious of the peril ahead, they walked right into the trap. It snapped shut at once. From their hiding-places spread out in the grass, the lions attacked at full charge, scattering the zebras, causing them to panic and flee in utter confusion. For a few moments there was total chaos, when a foal was separated from its mother and tripped up by a lioness. Immediately she fastened her teeth on its throat in a suffocating grip and before long the zebra took its last breath. The rest of the herd

escaped and now stared back at the lions from a safe distance, all flustered and whinnying like crazy.

While the lioness was still panting for breath next to the dead foal, the three pride males that had relaxed all morning under a tree and merely watched the five lionesses' hunting attempts, came charging up to her and grabbed the carcass from under her nose. With a disgusted snarl the female walked away, leaving her prey to the males. They sunk their teeth into the lifeless body and pulled at it with all their strength until it finally tore.

Usually these pride males are the best of friends, but in lion society kindness ends with matters of food. A fierce fight erupted between them over a dead zebra foal (above, left and page 23).

Like the rays of a star numerous game paths lead to and from a natural spring. Etosha is criss-crossed by countless game trails, etched deep into the earth by hooves and soles of animals commuting as they have for centuries between feeding grounds and water.

Disputing over territory and females, wildebeest bulls chase each other in a wild gallop at Okondeka spring. More than just a quick stopover for a drink, waterholes are a hub of activity, where there is time for lively play, for measuring each other's strength or for settling an occasional dispute.

Hundreds of springbok gather daily at the spring of Salvadora during the dry season (above). These highly adaptable antelopes, which also occur in the desert regions of Namibia, can survive long periods without drinking water, but when it is available springbok will drink every few days. As bulk feeders of low-quality grasses, Burchell's zebras, on the contrary, are extremely dependant on water (right and top right). In Etosha they drink almost daily and rarely move further than 15 kilometres from waterholes.

Etosha's lions are no threat to adult elephants (left), but will attack and kill youngsters if the opportunity arises. This, however, is rare, for elephant calves keep close to their mothers (right) and are well protected and fiercely defended by the herd against predators.

Page 28 and 29: Walking in single file, a breeding herd of elephants consisting of mothers and their offspring approaches a waterhole, where they may consume more than a thousand litres at a single visit. Small waterholes are often sucked dry by the time the pachyderms move off. Then, other wildlife is forced to either walk several kilometres to the next water point or to wait patiently until this waterhole fills up again.

In a rocking manner a group of giraffes walks gracefully across the Etosha plains (left). Towards dusk the herds get moving again. Giraffes, like wildebeest (above), zebras (right) and most other herbivores, abandon waterholes for safer sleeping grounds at night, as this is the time that predators often drink.

After marking its "sleeping tree", a male cheetah ends the day and begins its nightly rest (left). For the black-backed jackal (below) and the spotted hyena (right), however, sunset is the wake up call for a night of extended patrolling in search of prey or carcasses.

Seemingly out of nowhere a female leopard crouches down at the edge of the water and begins to drink peacefully. A few minutes later she sits up with a sudden movement, turns around and within seconds, is lost in the dark. Although they are probably quite common, leopards are rarely seen in Etosha because of their solitary, secretive way of life and perfect camouflage.

With a wild look that leaves no doubt that she won't take any nonsense, a lioness guards the carcass of a zebra. Although zebras and wildebeest are popular prey species, Etosha's lions mainly kill springbok, the most numerous antelope species in the Park.

Accompanied by much squabbling, black-backed jackals rip into a dead wildebeest calf. Mostly known as scavengers and hunters of birds and small mammals, the jackals of Etosha occasionally kill young antelopes, especially springbok lambs.

When most animals have left the waterholes for safety reasons, black rhinos (below) and elephants (left), the giants of Etosha, are on their way there for a sunset drink.

On her advance to a waterhole where another elephant herd is already drinking, an elephant cow raises her trunk in greeting. At dusk an inversion layer of air aids the travel of infrasound, low frequency calls not audible to the human ear, thus allowing elephants to communicate with each other over distances of more than 60 kilometres. In this way scattered herds of elephants may coordinate their arrival at a waterhole, a phenomenon that has puzzled scientists for some time.

Encounters between elephants and black rhinos, here a rhino mother with her offspring, are mostly uneventful. Generally the heavy weights have respect for each other and keep their distance. Occasionally, when they get too close to each other, a brusque threat pose is usually enough to avert a confrontation.

The meeting of black rhinos at a waterhole is often accompanied by much puffing and snorting – most of it part of amicable behaviour, followed by them drinking peacefully near each other. When they drink, rings form on the water, which are reflected by the flashlight and create peculiar patterns of stripes on the animals' bodies.

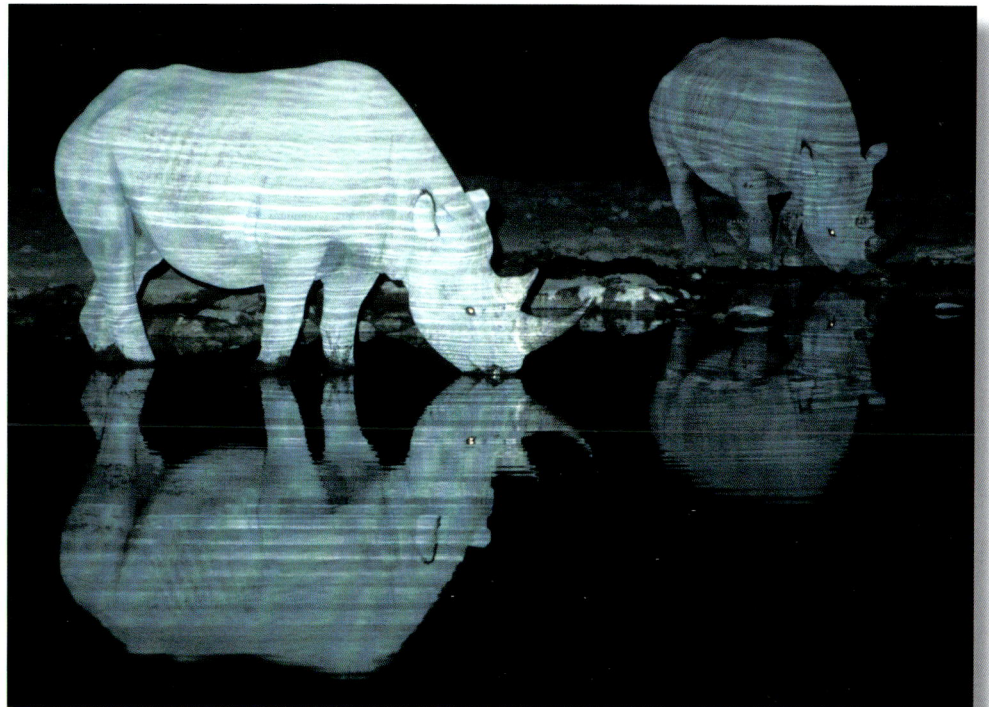

At dawn a lioness guards the rhino kill of the past night at Okaukuejo waterhole (left), while the three adult male lions that participated in the hunt, recover from the effort a short distance away. Generally black rhinos are safe from Etosha's lions, because the adults are quite aggressive and defend their calves vehemently against attackers. Sub-adult rhinos, however, which have just left their mothers and are still of relatively small body size, are occasionally killed by these predators. This group of male lions (below), which was also responsible for the rhino kill at Okaukuejo, has in the past killed several adolescent rhinos. With respect to the survival of the endangered black rhino, one has to hope that these cases remain exceptions.

At the M'Bari waterhole, the resident pride of lions was also seen on a rhino carcass some years ago. Fortunately this exotic meal seems to have been a single occurrence for that group of lions.

Having eaten their fill, some lionesses and lion cubs of the "M'Bari pride" drink in the first morning light. They are shy and sometimes aggressive towards humans, perhaps because part of the pride was shot on a farm south of the Park several years ago. Despite Etosha being fenced in, its lions occasionally venture onto neighbouring farmland, crawling under the fence where warthogs and porcupines have dug holes. There they are mostly unwelcome, for they kill farm stock and pose a threat to the farmers. Over the past 20 years nearly 600 lions have been killed by farmers and reported, but the actual number is thought to be much higher. Since 1980 Etosha's lion population has declined from an estimate of 500 to between 200 and 300 individuals. Nature conservationists are divided as to whether the population decline has been caused by too high losses on farmland, which would be of concern, or whether it lies within the frame of natural fluctuations.

Three months after the mating, which is often accompanied by aggressive growling, snarling and blows from her paw (above), the lioness gives birth to several blind and helpless cubs. At the age of one month when they are able to walk, the mother begins to lead them to her kills. She leaves her offspring behind during her hunting patrols and is greeted with exuberance upon her return (right). The cubs mostly remain well hidden in their lair, where they are relatively safe from other predators, especially spotted hyenas, which would kill them without hesitation. Sometimes, however, small lions forget themselves in their play and run about boisterously in the open (top right).

Stoically, an adult lioness (above) watches the wild play of sub-adult pride members (right, top right and far right). Most of Etosha's lions live in prides of between three to twelve members, occupying a defined hunting area around a waterhole and defending it against challengers. The foundation of lion society is the close social relationship between the mostly related pride females, especially the bond between mothers and daughters.

Lionesses that are born within a pride (right lion) generally remain there until death. The male offspring (left lion), however, leave the pride before three years of age, in part because the adult males do not tolerate them any longer. Lion males of the same litter often stay together after leaving the pride. At first they lead a nomadic existence until they finally, at the age of about five years, win a territory which includes the resident pride females.

An African wildcat lies motionless in a depression (left). Totally relying on the camouflage of her coat, she waits without any cover at the water's edge at Olifantsbad for the arrival of the Namaqua sandgrouse, that visit the waterholes daily. About an hour or two after sunrise the characteristic "kalke-ven"-calls announce the arrival of the first flocks. The birds land a few metres from the water, look around briefly and walk the short distance to the trough. Most of the sandgrouse distrust this strange rock and look for another spot to drink (top left), but some of them run obliviously towards the wildcat. Like a spring, the predatory cat jumps up and tries to snatch one of the birds from mid-air (above). After several unsuccessful attempts she finally has sandgrouse for breakfast.

Cheeky and clever hunters, black-backed jackals (top left) rarely miss an opportunity to stalk an inattentive ground squirrel, like this one (left) that stuffs its cheeks with the seeds of a dwarf shrub. At first the little rodent escapes into a near-by burrow, but it turns out to be a short tunnel with two entrances. When the jackal begins digging at the one hole, the squirrel flees through the other. However, the clever jackal has been expecting this move and snaps at once (above).

Towards the end of winter, in August and September, when day temperatures suddenly rise, nature performs one of its miracles: Without a single drop of rain having fallen, the leafless shrubs of the Acacia nebrownii put forth yellow, fragrant flowers (right). Due to their high content of nutritious proteins and sugars, giraffes (left), springbok (below), black-faced impalas and greater kudus consider them a delicacy and a welcome change from the wilted leaves of the other shrubs and trees.

Blending in with the dry leaves of the wintry mopane savanna (far left), a lioness looks out for prey, like a kudu female (left) and her kind, which are browsers and live in Etosha's dense tree savanna. More than half of the Park is covered with mopane, a wooded plant, which grows as a shrub or tree, depending on the condition of the soil. In July and August their butterfly-winged leaves, which make them easily recognizable (top left), change colour to brown and wilt before they are dropped in September. During this time elephants spurn mopane leaves, their main food in Etosha, and feed on the leaves, twigs and barks of the Acacia nebrownii shrubs (above) and other plants.

After a hot day, an elephant herd refreshes itself at a waterhole at dusk (left). The young ones obviously enjoy the "family outing" to the water very much (above) and use the opportunity for lively play and impetuous splashing around. To protect their skin against insects and drying out in the harsh sun, some elephants finally indulge in a dust bath (right) before the herd quietly and peacefully returns into the tree savanna.

Under the Relentless Sun

The Hot Dry Season

- September to December -

We listen to the still evening air.

Nothing. There is not the slightest sound coming from the procession of giants walking past, several tons heavy but quiet as mice. Their colossal silhouettes first move silently in front of the pink sunset sky, then fade in the dusty twilight before finally they are lost in the dark.

Since the late afternoon the breeding herd of ten elephants had been enjoying themselves at a waterhole. On their advance, the pachyderms at first trudged in a row with trunks raised, but on the last hundred metres they stormed to the water in sheer abandon, forgetting all discipline. Upon arrival, they eagerly sucked in the first litres of water with their trunks and sprayed them pleasurably into their mouths. Between the drinking giants, elephant calves pattered about excitedly. They only drank mother's milk and did not care much about the water. With floppy trunks and fluttering ears they chased each other, boisterously ramming each other in the sides and measuring their strength with head to head, high-spirited pushing.

The big ones obviously enjoyed the bathing trip too. Some sprayed their huge bodies energetically with trunk-loads of water; others waded into the pool, churning up the murky water by moving a leg vigorously back and forth to cool their massive bellies. One elephant cow decided to take a proper bath and submerged herself fully in the middle of the waterhole. Only now and then her trunk emerged, like a submarine periscope, cautiously breaking the surface for air, turning left, turning right, dropping again in slow motion and disappearing back into the water.

Eventually their exuberant drinking and bathing subsided and the waterhole became still again. For a few minutes the elephants stood motionless, like in a trance, then low rumbling sounds moved through the herd. This was the signal, a "let's go" rumble, whereupon the herd gathered and walked off peacefully, following a broad elephant path past us towards the sinking sun.

For several days a hot north-easterly wind has blown mercilessly. From the barren Etosha Pan the wind carries billions of fine clay particles, which spiralling high into the sky form a huge dust plume. To the west and south of the Pan storms of thick white dust sweep across the savanna, swallowing landmarks, muffling sound and blowing away smells. Deprived of life-saving warning signals the animals are visibly uneasy. Huddled together, groups of springbok, Burchell's zebra and blue wildebeest stand anxiously in the howling wind, waiting for the storm to die down. Finally, while the elephants bath in the early evening, the wind subsides. Dust still lingers in the air as quietness settles across the land.

It is the height of the dry season. For several months the sun has been beating down relentlessly from a cloudless sky, with temperatures occasionally climbing above 40 degrees Celsius. During the sweltering midday heat most living things, including us humans, doze exhaustedly, for the slightest movement is too taxing. Towards the evening the heat finally eases off, and a sigh of relief wafts across the land. The animals slowly awaken from their daze and begin to feed well into the night.

Lately, however, the search for food has become more arduous. Months of incessant drought have transformed the savanna into a desolate wasteland. Most grass of the past rainy season has been eaten, trampled or blown away by the winds. The little that is left has been sucked dry to lifeless, pale stalks. The leaves of trees and shrubs are now also withered and low in nutrients or have dropped altogether. More and more often thirst drives the weak animals back to the dwindling waterholes. In this hard and extreme time, life in Etosha becomes a struggle close to the edge of survival.

When all creatures groan under the heat and dryness, relief is on its way: over night moist air rolls in from the north-east, as far away as Angola and Zambia, spreading the smell of distant rain. Like a fleet of historic ships in full sail, white cumulus clouds line the horizon and wake the memory of a long-cherished dream. As if afraid to draw near, the clouds hang in the distance for days, only now and then sending ahead the odd messenger. It sails closer hesitantly and evaporates slowly, dissolving into thin air. One morning, however, the clouds have disappeared from the horizon as suddenly as they have appeared. With them the dream of the beginning of the longed-for rainy season is gone.

Days, sometimes only weeks later, the ghostlike clouds are back. This time they move closer, cautiously, assembling in scattered groups and growing into towering mountains of clouds. Towards evening they turn into menacing thunderclouds and after dark, streaks of lightening flash through the night. Where they hit the ground, the completely bone-dry vegetation catches fire instantly, burning like tinder. Strengthened by the wind and fuelled by the dry grass, the flames spread fast, devouring the foliage and branches close to the ground and sometimes even whole trees. Despite leaving a trail of destruction, the fire creates space and the ashes provide important minerals for the beginning of new plant growth.

At last the thunderclouds burst. Before reaching the ground, however, the rain often evaporates in the hot air, and the savanna remains dry. Here, the promise is finally fulfilled: large, heavy drops hit the parched land and the dream of rain becomes a reality. The next morning the storm clouds are gone. The sun conquers the sky again, and with her the unrelenting heat returns. In areas, where sufficient rain has fallen, fresh green grass springs up within a few days. As if called by the inaudible voices of promising rain clouds and the scent of verdant savanna, hundreds of springbok, wildebeest and zebras arrive and eagerly feed their fill. But the fortune does not last long. Soon the soil dries out and the grass wilts under the scorching sun. The animals move on and the wait for the relieving rainy season continues.

An ostrich couple waits anxiously for a storm to abate (left). In September and October hot winds frequently blow from the north-east. Where they sweep across barren land they transform into short-lived, localized sand storms. When blue wildebeest (above), elephants (page 55) and other herbivores leave the waterholes towards sunset, the wind dies down, but hours later the dust still lingers.

In the midday heat dust-laden whirlwinds, so-called "dust devils", develop in many places on the Etosha Pan. When moving across the open surface of the Pan, they swirl loose particles in a spiral, hundreds of metres up into the air. As soon as they hit dense vegetation or when the wind eases off, they lose momentum and disperse.

Countless Burchell's zebras and blue wildebeest come to the spring of Okondeka during the hot dry season (left). Heat and constant dryness drive the wildlife to the remaining waterholes more and more often. At certain springs and boreholes the water surface shrinks to a few square metres because of the intense animal pressure, and only a few animals may drink at the same time. Many of the thirsty animals that have gathered at the waterhole during the course of the day wait for hours, sometimes even until dusk for a chance to drink (above).

Feigning a vast lake, the cloudless sky above Etosha reflects on the great, barren Pan. In desert climates bizarre mirages develop when the bottom layers of air heat up excessively. Giraffes (above), wildebeest (far right), springbok (right) and other wildlife take a short cut across the Etosha Pan to get to water, despite ground temperatures of more than 50 degrees Celsius.

An elephant's trunk is a power pack of more than 10 000 individual muscles. Having evolved from the nose and upper lip, it can hold about six litres of water and serves as an important organ of touch. It is strong enough to push down a tree and sensitive enough to pick up a single flower.

Elephants love water. During the hot season they spend hours at waterholes in order to cool down their massive bodies, which cannot give off heat easily. With strong pulls of their trunks, they suck up lukewarm water by the litre and spray it onto their bellies (far left). Their favourite pastime, however, is to take a bath, either peacefully all by themselves (right) or combined with playful wrestling with another elephant (below).

Warthogs have their own
strategies to bear the heat.
Between refreshing mud baths
(left), which are followed
by scratch massages at an
old tree stump (below), they
simply rest to save energy
(right).

Accompanied by deafening twittering, redbilled queleas, occasionally occurring in swarms of millions of birds, land in a tree. Weak branches and leaves break under their weight, but at the same time their dung is deposited on the ground and provides the tree with important nutrients.

In synchronized flight the swarm of redbilled queleas moves across the dry savanna like a dark cloud, continuously changing its shape (above and right). Incessant chirping and the rustling of wings announce their arrival from far away. The noise stops briefly when the redbilled queleas descend onto a waterhole and drink on the wing (left). Seconds later the cloud of birds lifts back into the air and moves off noisily.

In the hot dry season, extensive walks in search for food and frequent visits at the waterholes are everyday life for Etosha's herbivores (bottom left and above). Although wildlife has adapted to the intense heat, because of the lack of nutrients and shortage in food, some animals, especially the ill and injured, are at the edge of survival (top left).

The death of an animal does not remain undiscovered for long. Whitebacked vultures (below) are generally the first to spot carcasses from the air, but black-backed jackals (left), spotted hyenas (bottom left) and lions also track down dead animals quickly with their acute sense of smell.

Within a few days whitebacked vultures, the most common vulture in Etosha, have stripped a zebra carcass to the bone (above and right). Often referred to as the "garbage removers" of the savanna, scavengers play an important role within the ecosystem. They get rid of carcasses of animals that have succumbed to diseases against which they are immune.

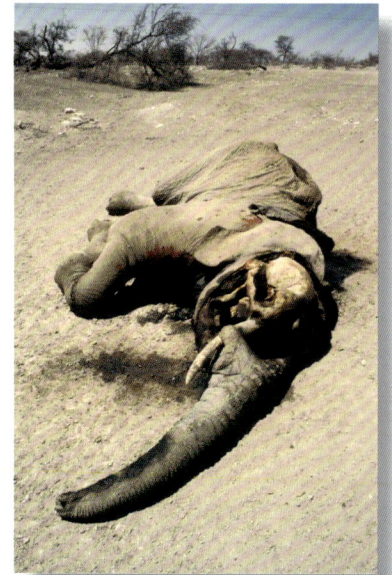

Every year during the hot dry season (above) numerous elephants die of anthrax (right). The disease also affects zebras, springbok and wildebeest, which succumb to it especially towards the end of the rainy season. Animals contract the disease by picking up anthrax spores, survival forms of the bacteria, which may lie dormant for centuries. Scientists believe anthrax spores may enter the animal through abrasions in the mouth and throat. Once the bacteria take over the body's defenses, death is inevitable.

Many hungry mouths can gorge themselves at an elephant carcass. When an individual lion, which is too weak to hunt because of illness (above) or old age (right), can feed undisturbed for days on a huge carcass, it often regains its strength and escapes death.

Promising rain clouds appear in the sky, the humidity rises and all life groans under the muggy heat. Towards the evening individual showers may fall, but the rain often evaporates in the air and the parched landscape remains dry (below). At last, somewhere a storm breaks and drenches the earth in a small area. Zebras (left), wildebeest (right) and springbok follow the promising clouds and feed on the fresh green grass that soon sprouts. A few days later the sun beats down again from the clear blue sky, the plants wither, the puddles dry up and the animals move on.

Followed by low rolling thunder, dazzling lightning electrifies the black cloudbank of a nightly, localized thunderstorm. Where lightning strikes, the dry vegetation catches fire at once. Nourished by the wind, it whips through the parched landscape with great speed (left). Nearly every year towards the end of the dry season natural bush fires occur in Etosha. They play an important role in the ecology of the African savanna because they remove dead plant material, create space for new growth, and the ash provides important nutrients (below and right).

Etosha now resembles a desert. With the exception of the green mopane trees, which sprout new leaves in October without a drop of rain, everything is grey, dusty and dried out towards the end of the year (left). When all hope for relief seems lost, the miracle happens at last: From the north-east, clouds heavy with rain roll in and darken the sky above Etosha (below), condensing until finally they explode in magnificent storms (right). The rainy season has begun.

Clouds of Mercy

The Rainy Season

- January to April -

Laughing and cheering

amid the swamped savanna we celebrate the miracle that has emerged from the storm. With a soft gurgle the water around us slowly flows towards lower terrain. The cool air is invigorating, the smell of rain and wet earth beguiling. Above us the veil of clouds has been lifting steadily after the heavy rainstorm. On the horizon the thunderclouds are still raging, now and then flashing from lightning within and rumbling in a low bass. Suddenly sunlight breaks through the western sky and pours a symphony of colours onto this rare, translucent water world, as if bidding the dry season farewell and announcing the beginning of the rainy season.

The rain has changed everything. The air is clear and moist, the temperature pleasant. Washed clean of the white dust of the dry season, the savanna gleams in pastel earth colours and glistens with pools and puddles. Here the wildlife drinks at leisure, ignoring the perennial waterholes, which lie deserted. Quiet nights now come to life with termites, moths as well as other hatched insects buzzing and fluttering about with bats and nightjars chasing after them in a feeding frenzy.

The most significant transformation, though, is happening quietly within the soaked soil. Seeds, that have lain dormant for months, maybe years, germinate and sprout, and within a few days breathe life onto the pale land with a timid tinge of green: it is grass, the lifeblood of the African savanna. Soon the plains are dotted with Burchell's zebras, blue wildebeest and springbok. With heads low and moving incessantly, they cut the grass with their sharp incisors, finally eating their fill after the past harsh months.

Meanwhile a flood is quietly on its way towards Etosha. Fed by rains further north and east, the ephemeral rivers of the Ekuma, Oshigambo and Omuramba Owambo – most of the year dry riverbeds – are running. In good years the waters reach as far as the Etosha Pan, where they form wide bodies of water at the mouths. The flooding Omuramba Owambo first fills Fisher's Pan, an eastern extension of the Etosha Pan, before it overflows into the main pan. Thousands of waterbirds arrive to feast on small fish, water insects and countless micro-organisms that have made the journey with the water. Together with fairy shrimps, tadpole shrimps and blue-green algae that now appear in vast numbers, they form a rich food supply.

Waders, among them blackwinged stilts and pied avocets, gracefully strut about in the shallows; grey herons stand motionless in the water, in wait for frogs or little fish swimming past; Cape teals and red-billed teals paddle about cheekily, nibbling on small aquatic plants and insects; greater and lesser flamingos, at times gathering in the thousands, wade about on long reddish legs, honking and chattering endlessly.

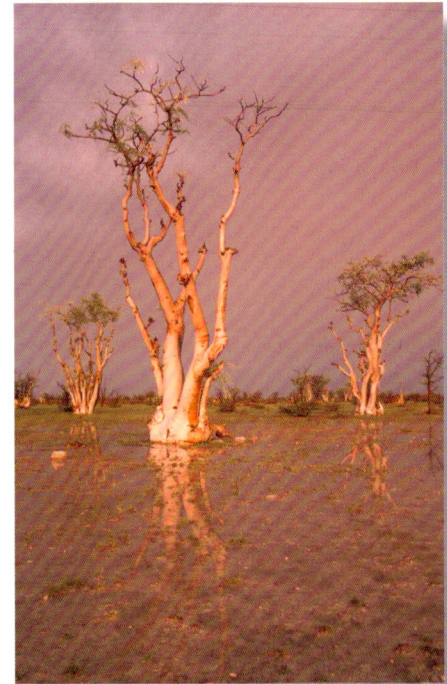

With the onset of the rainy season, a wave of restlessness spills across the park, seizing springbok, wildebeest and zebras. Herd after herd begins its traditional migration to the grass plains west of the Etosha Pan. Soon merging into large groups, which move in long files, their march mushrooms into a large procession. For a pride of lions that has settled along their route, the moving animals – many of them heavily pregnant – provide easy pickings. After a few days the first herds finally arrive at their favourite summer grazing area. It was quiet here during the dry season for there is no permanent water, but now the grassland comes to life and echoes with the whinnying, lowing and grunting of thousands of animals.

One morning a springbok ewe rests, a little separated from the herd, beside her a tiny wet bundle is lying motionless. She reaches back to her new-born lamb and for a second, mother and young touch noses for the very first time. While the ewe begins to lick its coat clean, the tiny springbok stirs and, only minutes old, tries to get up. The first few attempts fail, its legs give way and it tumbles back onto the grass, but soon the lamb stands for a few seconds on long, wobbly legs. A little later it takes its first unsteady steps towards its mother, where it instantly searches for her teats and takes its first drink. Within a few hours it is sturdy enough to run beside its mother if they must flee from a predator. In the coming weeks hundreds of other springbok lambs, wildebeest calves and zebra foals will be born into this time of plenty. In mixed herds they romp carefree amid the lush grass carpet dotted with yellow flowers.

For a few weeks Etosha is a paradise on earth, where food and water are available in abundance. This is a precious time for renewal and for regaining strength. Eventually, however, hardly noticed at first, the clouds vanish from the sky. In the absence of replenishing rains, the ephemeral lakes and short-lived puddles quickly dry up, causing migratory birds to leave for wetter realms, and the wildlife to gradually return to the winter grazing areas and congregate at permanent waterholes again.

At dusk we watch a herd of springbok grazing on the yellowing grass plains, when a little springbok suddenly races off and begins to bounce around like a rubber ball, with lowered head, arched back and stiffened legs. At once others join in and soon the entire herd leaps up and down boisterously in a wildly choreographed dance of celebration. Although "pronking", as this behaviour is called, might serve as practice for predator evasive action, to us, it simply looks like high spirits and exuberance at being alive. The rainy season is over, but Etosha is strengthened and prepared for the coming dry season.

Lightning flashes wildly as the thunderstorm continues to rage in the distance, meanwhile silence has settled over the moringa trees of the "fairytale forest" (left and page 81). Rapidly soaking Etosha's savanna and grass plains (above), heavy storms are characteristic of the rainy season. They are followed by rainless periods of several days, during which the sky clears, the flooded landscape slowly dries up and pleasantly warm days encourage plant growth.

When the first strong rains transform dusty depressions into ponds (right), the underlying soil softens and bullfrogs awaken from their "dry season rest" in cavities within the soil. Emerging from the mud, suddenly hundreds of frogs romp about in the pools (below). Bullfrogs are the largest frog species in southern Africa. The adult males are bigger than the females and reach a considerable length of 20 centimetres. Eating anything that moves, the nocturnal bullfrogs' diet ranges from small birds, mice and insects to scorpions, snakes and other frogs, including their own kind.

Grey herons (above) and numerous other water birds soon arrive, eager to take advantage of the proliferation of bullfrogs and other amphibians.

After the first good rains, insect life suddenly awakens. Termites leave their nests for their nuptial flight in order to establish a new colony (above), while moths, grasshoppers, beetles and flies as well as numerous other insects suddenly fill the moist air.

Following the clouds, flocks of Abdim's storks arrive in Etosha at the beginning of the rainy season. During the day they eat their fill of delicacies from the abundant supply of insects (far left). Shortly before sunset, the storks settle one after the other on suitable sleeping trees (left). Accompanied by hoarse hissing and wild flapping of their wings, the birds fight for the best sleeping spots (above). After dark they finally settle and peace descends.

Etosha is now also a paradise for bat-eared foxes,
which mainly eat insects, spiders and scorpions.
With their excellent hearing and sense of smell they
can detect the larvae of insects within the soil (left).
Born shortly before the start of the rainy season,
their young cubs eat their fill on the rich food supply
(below and right).

Menacing grey-black storm clouds brew in the sky, before a localized and heavy thundershower finally breaks (left). Turned away from the wind, blue wildebeest (above), springbok (right) and other animals stand motionless and huddled in the rain. This behaviour prevents their bodies from cooling down too rapidly.

Like most cats, cheetahs usually shy away from water. These two (left), however, take advantage of the rain for a surprise attack (top right) on a herd of springbok standing huddled in the rain (below). Fleeing in panic, the antelopes narrowly escape the predatory cats (bottom right).

While a storm front draws near, zebras peacefully graze on the green grass plains west of the Etosha Pan (above and right). Thousands of zebras, wildebeest and springbok from other parts of the Park marched for several days to feed on the fresh, juicy grasses of these favourite summer grazing areas.

When animals gather in large herds, lions are soon to follow. Between their nightly hunts, which are mostly successful with such vast animal numbers (below), the mighty cats relax lazily in the grass for up to twenty hours a day (left and right).

Dusty and dry riverbeds during the dry season, the Oshigambo (left) and the Ekuma (below) may flow after heavy rain falls to the north of Etosha. In good years of rain, they reach the Etosha Pan and form large sweet water lakes at their mouths. Local showers over Etosha fill a prehistoric river course on the Etosha Pan (right). In unusually wet years, the Pan is transformed into an ephemeral, shallow lake.

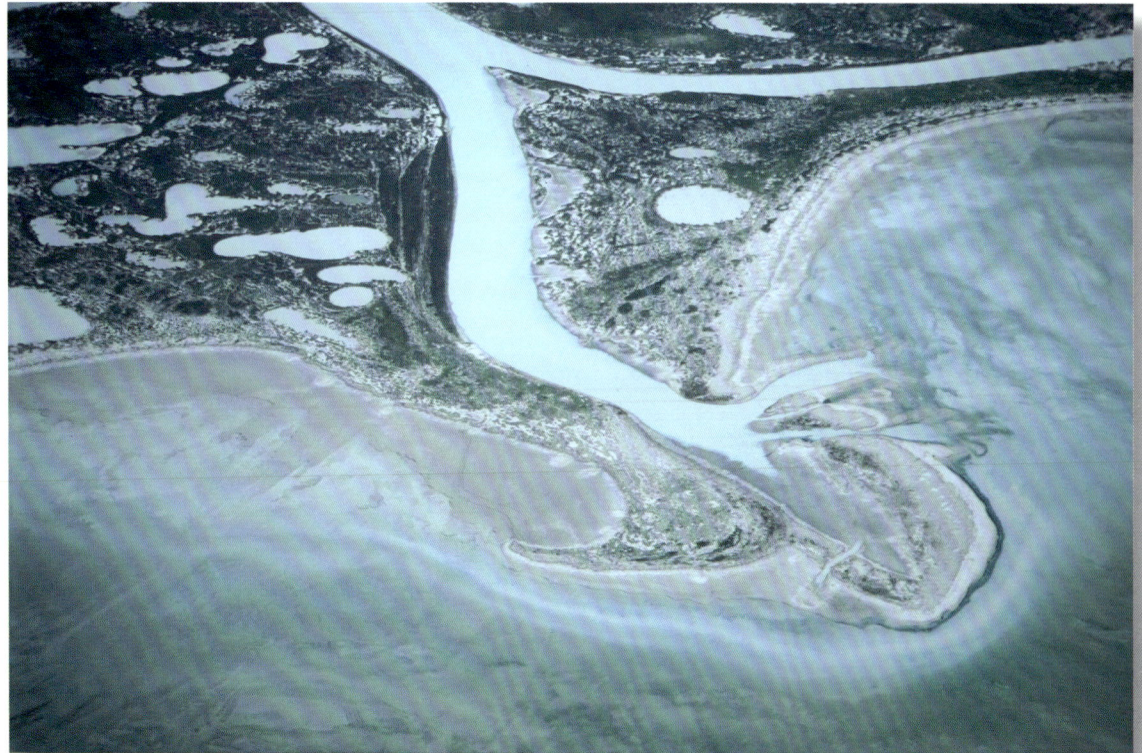

At the start of the rainy season in northern Namibia, greater and lesser flamingos often leave their winter homes at Namibia's coastal lagoons, particularly Sandwich Harbour and Walvis Bay, to head for inland wetlands (left). Thousands of flamingos visit Etosha because of the rich food supply and, in some years, to breed here. In southern Africa the Etosha Pan and the Makgadikgadi Pan in Botswana are the main mass breeding sites for both species of flamingos.

The breeding colonies of greater and lesser flamingos are often intermixed and, as protection against predators, they lie mostly far out on the Etosha Pan (right). While some greater flamingos have already settled on one of their traditional breeding sites (circle of birds), other greater and lesser flamingos are still busy with preparations. Although flamingos nest on the Etosha Pan every few years, most breeding attempts are unsuccessful. Chicks only hatch after 28 days of incubation and take another two and a half months before they are fully fledged. Water around the colonies often subsides before the chicks are able to leave with their parents. The abandoned brood has little chance of survival.

Each year, lured by a rich supply of water insects, crustaceans, molluscs and blue-green algae, hundreds of greater flamingos (left) and lesser flamingos (below) visit Fisher's Pan, an eastern extension of the Etosha Pan which is flooded by the Omuramba Owambo. Staying anywhere from several months to several weeks, the birds return to the Atlantic coast once the water has dried up towards the end of the rainy season.

Away from the herd, a springbok ewe lies down to bear her lamb (left). Silently and inconspicuously she pushes her young further and further out, until just twenty minutes later, it lies motionless in the grass. For a few seconds both lie still from exhaustion, then the mother reaches back to her lamb and their noses touch for the very first time (middle). Soon the little springbok attempts to get up (below), but falls back to the ground again and again while the ewe licks it clean (right). She even eats the afterbirth to remove all traces of smell that could attract a predator. Within a few hours the lamb is sturdy enough on its legs to flee from danger.

Seeking protection, wildebeest calves press against their mothers during a thundershower (above). This prevents the calves from cooling off too much in the cold rain. Thousands of blue wildebeest and springbok give birth within a few weeks of the onset of the rainy season. Other herbivores, like Burchell's zebras (right) and black-faced impalas (far right), also have their young in the rainy season when an abundance of food and water promises the best start for a new life.

A sea of yellow Tribulus (left) and Hirpicium (below) flowers brings additional colour onto the green savanna. Particularly on overgrazed soils these annual flowering plants dominate the landscape within a few days of the first rains. On sandy soils Sesamum flowers provide spots of pink (right).

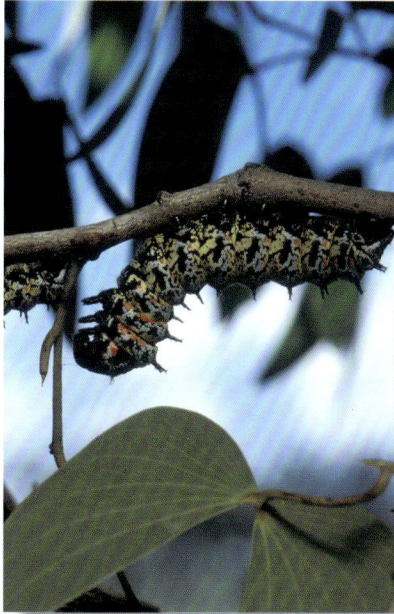

"Mopane worms" (above and left), which are actually caterpillars, seem to have an insatiable appetite. These Emperor moth larvae grow to approximately seven centimetres in length and can be as thick as a man's finger. The moths lay their eggs at the beginning of the rainy season and after hatching "en masse", the caterpillars strip large areas of mopane forest of its leaves within weeks. At the same time, they produce vast amounts of natural fertilizer, which benefits the mopane trees (right). For numerous birds, insects and even for the human inhabitants of Etosha, mopane worms are protein-rich delicacies. Even after they have buried themselves in the ground and pupated, mopane worms are dug out and eaten by jackals, bat-eared foxes and even by warthogs.

When the grasses finally produce seeds (left), good times begin for helmeted guineafowls (above) and other seed-eaters that have to provide for their offspring now. While one of the last thundershowers goes down in the distance, fields of lush grass sway in the warm wind after a good rainy season (right). This is the food supply of Etosha's grazers for the following eight months of dry season. It must last until the next rainy season sets in again.

Finally the rain stops all together. The sun shines from a cloudless sky and soon the pools are dry. Zebras (left), wildebeest and springbok return to their winter feeding grounds near the perennial waterholes (below) where lions also gather (right and far right). The rainy season has ended, but Etosha's wildlife is strengthened and prepared for the long, hard dry season ahead.

Epilogue

The many years we spent in Etosha have been some of the best in our lives so far. During this time the wilderness revealed many of its secrets to us and taught us important things about ourselves. Living in Etosha meant to live in accordance with the rhythms of nature: together with the wild animals we enjoyed the cool winter months, suffered during the relentlessly hot and dusty dry season and breathed a sigh of relief when the rainy season finally began. Whenever we observed Etosha's animals, a feeling of tranquillity and happiness flowed through us, and we felt one with nature. Etosha awakened a deep fascination and respect in us of untouched wildness, of the powerful forces of nature and of the grandness of creation.

At the same time we were quite concerned, because the existence of the Etosha National Park and other wilderness areas is no guarantee for the future. With the land hunger of the ever growing world population, nature can end up in dire straits. Every day huge areas of pristine landscapes are being destroyed and are lost forever.

But there is hope. In many places national parks and other areas of nature make much higher profits through growing worldwide tourism, than any other form of land use. Thus, nature gains considerable economic worth. In a world, in which the economy seems to be the driving force, this is good news.

There is also another reason, why the wildernesses of this earth should be preserved for us and for the coming generations. We think, that man is part of nature and needs it for his psychological well-being. Time spent at one with nature is pure therapy, which uplifts the spirit and creates a feeling of peace and happiness. The wilderness reminds us, that there are still things in the world, which are greater than us, wild and indomitable – and this does the soul good.

Gallery

Claudia with a tranquillized radio-collared lion

Back from a field trip

Enjoying the full moon over the Etosha Pan

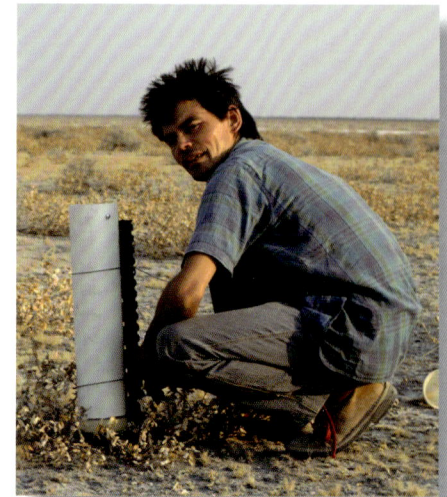
Wynand puts up a rain-gauge

Our adopted baby squirrel "Sprokies"

Claudia with the bull-frogs

Waiting for "the shot"

We are stuck ! Wynand after six hours of digging us out

Wynand locates animals carrying radio-collars

Playing with an adopted young genet

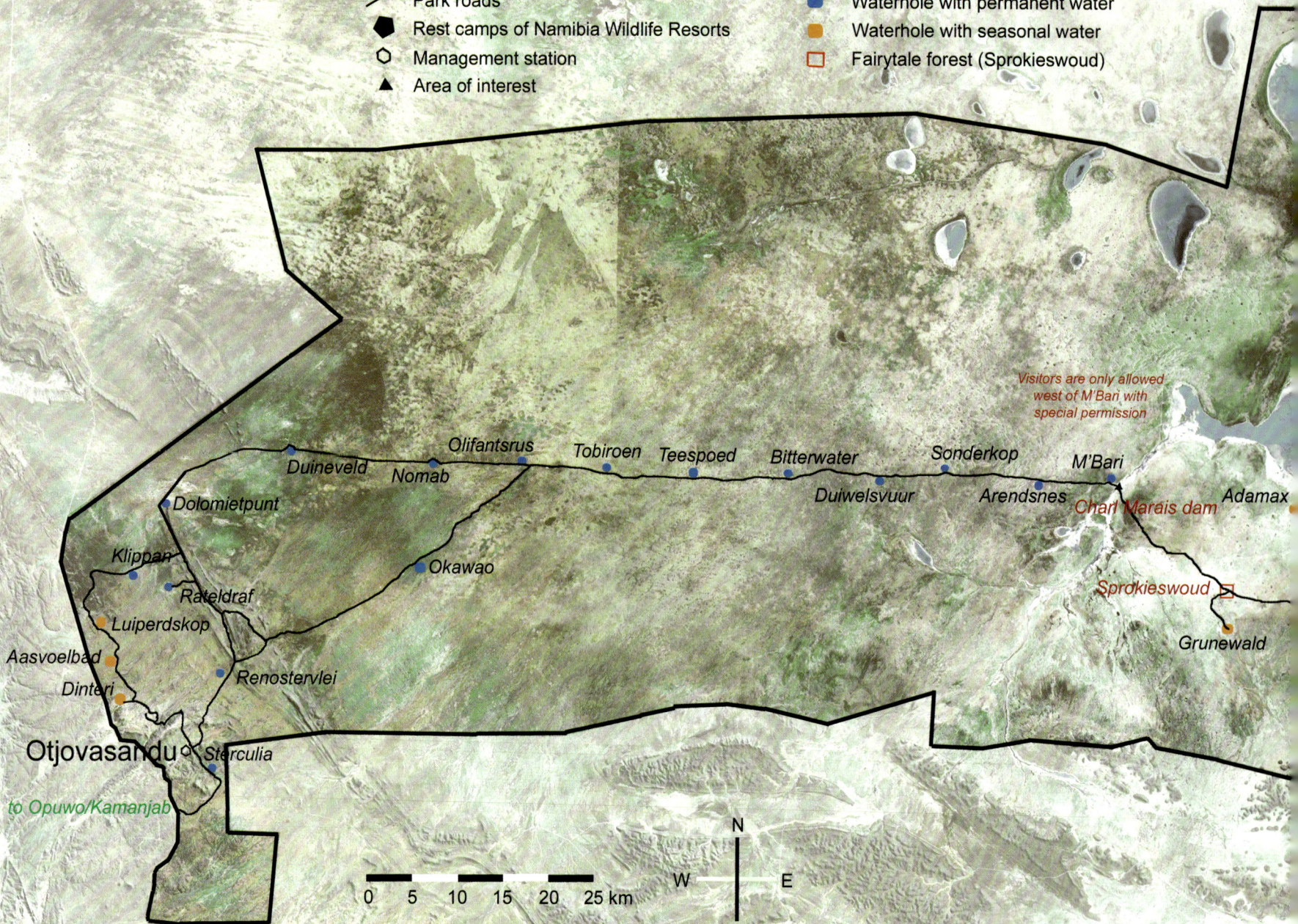

Satellite image and visitors' road map of the Etosha National Park

(Sources: NASA/Earthsat, Etosha Ecological Institute)

Park roads

Rest camps of Namibia Wildlife Resorts

Management station

Area of interest

Waterhole with permanent water

Waterhole with seasonal water

Fairytale forest (Sprokieswoud)

Visitors are only allowed west of M'Bari with special permission

Duineveld

Nomab

Olifantsrus

Tobiroen

Teespoed

Bitterwater

Duiwelsvuur

Sonderkop

Arendsnes

M'Bari

Adamax

Charl Marais dam

Dolomietpunt

Klippan

Rateldraf

Luiperdskop

Okawao

Sprokieswoud

Aasvoelbad

Dinteri

Renostervlei

Grunewald

Otjovasandu

Sterculia

to Opuwo/Kamanjab

0 5 10 15 20 25 km

N
W   E
S

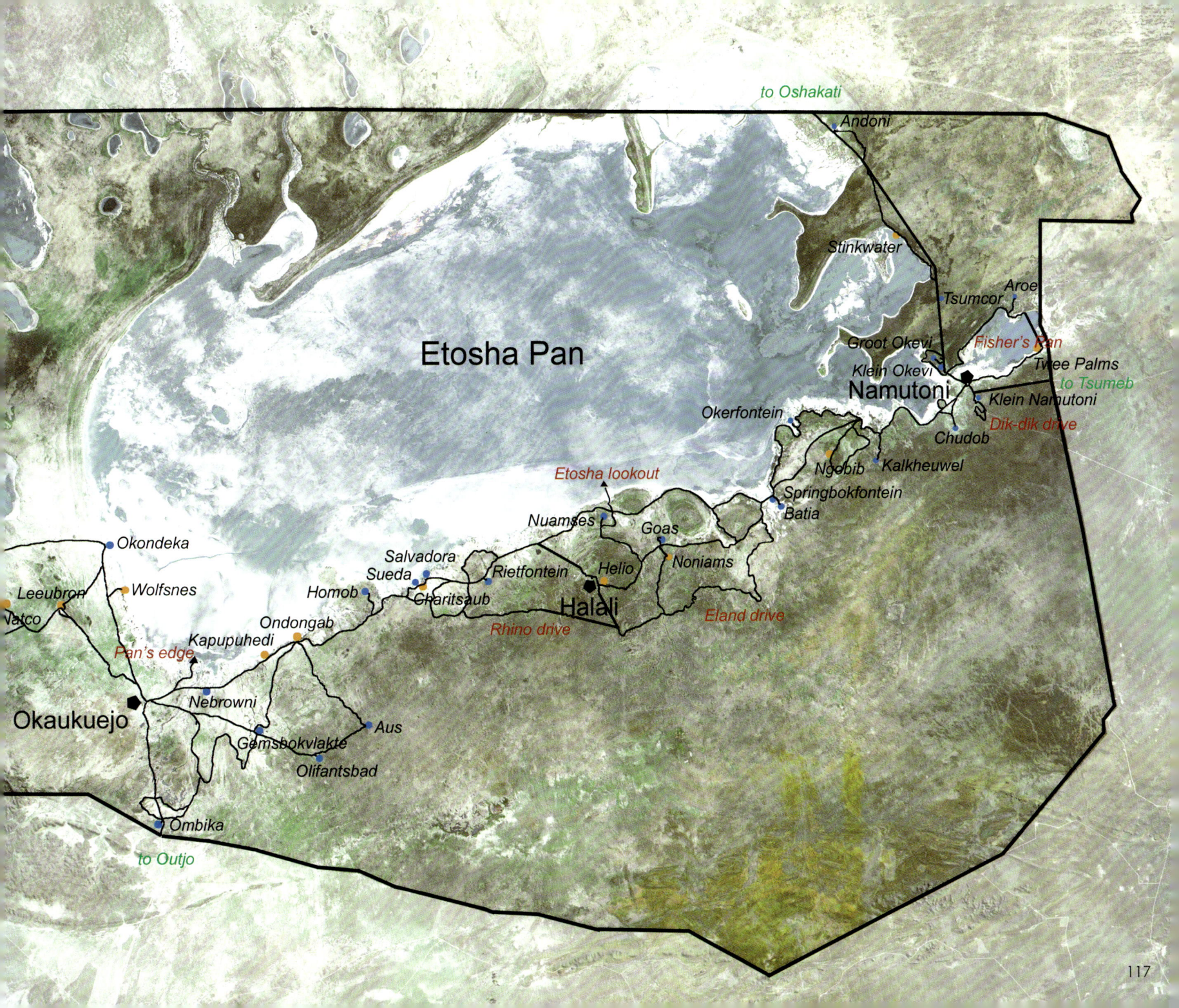

Etosha Pan

to Oshakati

Andoni

Stinkwater

Aroe

Tsumcor

Groot Okevi

Fisher's Pan

Klein Okevi

Twee Palms

Namutoni

to Tsumeb

Klein Namutoni

Okerfontein

Dik-dik drive

Chudob

Ngobib

Kalkheuwel

Etosha lookout

Springbokfontein

Batia

Nuamses

Goas

Noniams

Salvadora

Helio

Sueda

Rietfontein

Charitsaub

Halali

Eland drive

Homob

Rhino drive

Okondeka

Ondongab

Leeubron

Wolfsnes

Kapupuhedi

Natco

Pan's edge

Nebrowni

Aus

Okaukuejo

Gemsbokvlakte

Olifantsbad

Ombika

to Outjo

Imprint

Title: Etosha, Rhythms of an African Wilderness

Photographs: Claudia & Wynand du Plessis

Text: Claudia du Plessis

Layout, Desktop Publishing (DTP) and Artwork: Wynand du Plessis

Publishers: Claudia & Wynand du Plessis

ISBN: 978-99916-63-14-2

EAN: 978-9991663142

First publised: 2003

Second revised edition: 2007 - Printed in South Africa

www.claudiawynandduplessis.com

The authors guarantee that the photographs in this book are original images that have not been digitally manipulated. Only the cover photograph has been digitally extended at its top and bottom edge to fit the book format.

Photographic credits:

l. = left , r. = right , m. = middle , t. = top , b. = bottom

Images by Claudia du Plessis:

1, 2, 4, 5, 7, 10, 11, 14 b., 16 l., 18 t.l. & b.r. & b.m. & b.l., 19 t.r. & b.r. & b.m. & b.l., 20 t., 22, 23, 24, 25, 26 b., 27 t.r., 31, 32, 33 b., 34 l. & r., 36, 37 b., 38 t., 40 b., 43 t.r. & b., 44 l. & t.r. & b.r., 45, 46 b., 47 t.l. & b., 50 l., 51, 53 t.l., 55, 56, 58 t. & b., 59, 62 l. & r., 63 t. & b., 64 t. & b., 65, 66 l., 67 b., 68 l., 70 b.l., 71 t., 74 t. & b., 75, 78 t., 79, 81, 83, 84 r., 86 b.m., 88 t. & b., 89, 90, 91 t. & b., 93 t., 94 t. & b., 95 l. & t.r., 98 t., 99 b., 100 t.l. & m.l. & b.r., 101, 103 r., 104 t., 105, 107 l. & r., 108 r., 110 b., 112, 113, 114 t.r. & b.l., 115 t.r. & b.m. & b.l., large photo back cover;

Images by Wynand du Plessis:

Cover photo, -1, 0, 6, 9, 12, 13 t. & r. & b., 14 t., 15, 16 r., 17, 18 t.m. & t.r. & m.l., 19 t.l. & t.m., 20 b., 21, 26 t., 27 t.l. & b., 28/29, 30, 33 t., 35, 37 t., 38 b., 39 t. & b., 40 t., 41, 42, 43 t.l., 46 t.l. & t.r., 47 t.r., 48 l. & r., 49, 50 t.r. & b.r., 52, 53 b.r., 54, 57, 60 t. & b., 61, 66 r., 67 t., 68 r., 69, 70 t.l. & m.r., 71 b., 72 l. & r., 73 t. & b., 76 l. & r., 77, 78 b., 80, 82, 84 l., 85, 86 t.l. & b.r., 87, 92 t. & b., 93 b., 95 b.r., 96 t. & b., 97, 98 b., 99 t., 102, 103 l., 104 b., 106, 108 l., 109, 110 t., 111 l. & r., 114 t.l. & m. & b.r., 115 t.l. & b.r.;